Musical Munchies
Song Book

Frances Turnbull

Copyright © 2017 Frances Turnbull

Musical Munchies Song Book
All rights reserved
Musicaliti Publishing, Bolton, UK

ISBN: 978-1907935787

www.musicaliti.co.uk

Contents

Ukulele Tuning and Chords	5
Andy Pandy	7
Ally Bally Bee	9
Round and Round	11
Jolly Miller	13
Lemonade	15
Ten Green Bottles	17
Ickle Ockle	19
Five Fat Sausages	21
Apple Tree	23
Apple Peaches Chant	25
Hot Cross Buns	27
Five Currant Buns	29
Come Butter	31
Muffin Man	33
Oranges and Lemons	35
Paw Paw Patch	37
Skip to my Lou	39
Pumpkin pumpkin	41
Pease Pudding	43
Oats, Peas, Beans	45
Write your own song	47

Musical Munchies Song Book

Ukulele Chords

Ukuleles are small, accessible and relatively cheap instruments that can be used to play the accompaniment to many songs.

Each string should be tuned to specific notes (can be found on tuned instruments like xylophones, pianos or recorders etc.). The standard ukulele tuning is:

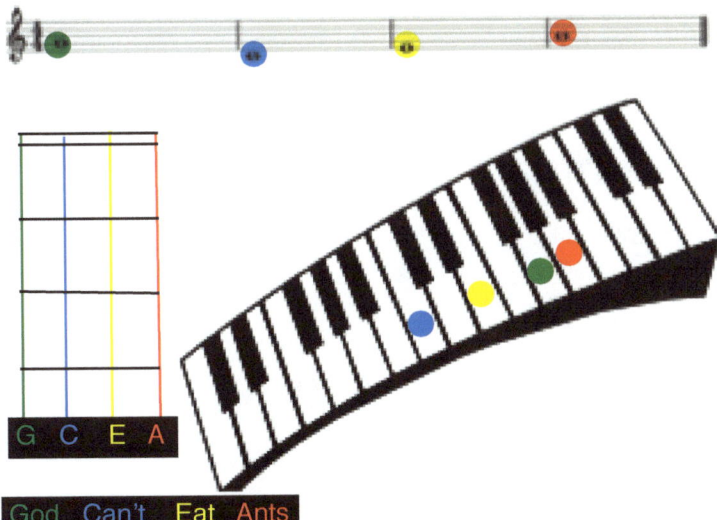

G C E A
God Can't Eat Ants

By placing your fingers on the frets at the positions on the pictures, (between the lines), you change the sound of the strings into chords when strummed altogether.

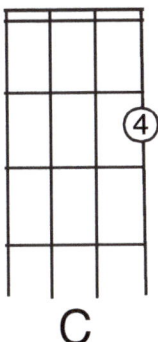
C

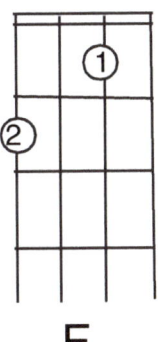
F

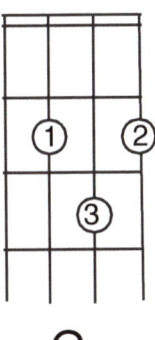
G

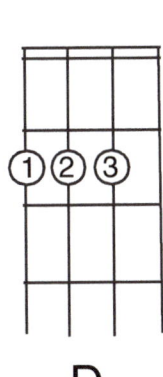
D

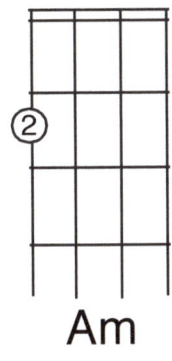
Am

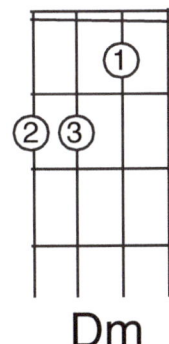
Dm

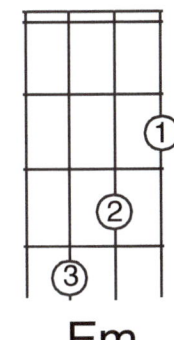
Em

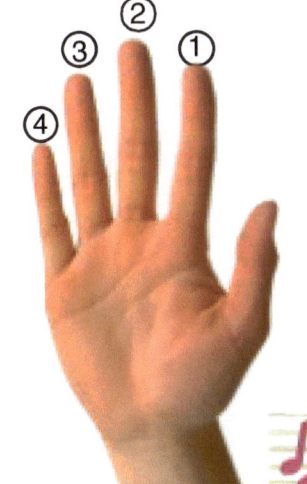

Marshmallow Crispy Squares

Ingredients:

50g butter

1 teaspoon vanilla extract

200g marshmallows

100g crisped rice cereal

Method:

1. Grease a 22x33cm (9x13 in) tin with oil or butter.
2. In a large saucepan, melt the butter over low heat.
3. Add the vanilla.
4. Melt the marshmallows into the butter, stirring.
5. Add the cereal when the marshmallows have melted; stir until cereal is coated.
6. Quickly pour into the prepared tin.
7. Use a sheet of greaseproof paper to press the mixture down flat and evenly into the tin.
8. Let set for 2 to 3 hours. Cut into squares.

Frances Turnbull

Andy Pandy

Traditional

[C] Andy Pandy sugar and candy all jump [F] up

[C] Andy Pandy sugar and candy all jump [F] down

[C] Andy Pandy sugar and candy all jump [F] in

[C] Andy Pandy sugar and candy all jump [G] out [C]

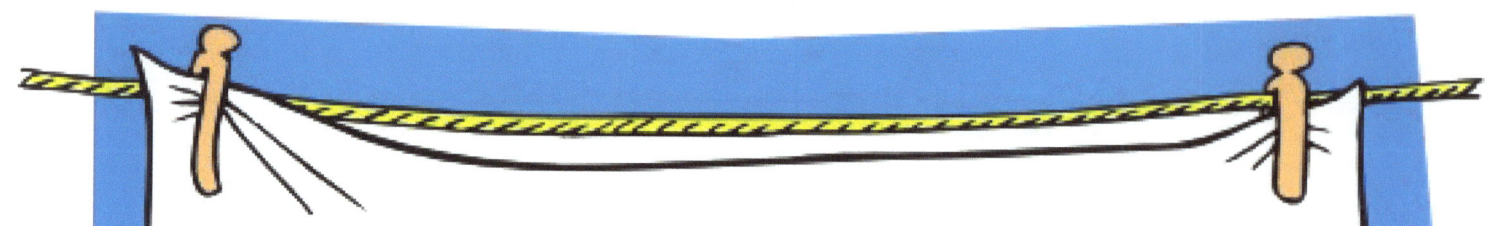

No-cook Peppermint Creams

Ingredients:

1 egg white

340g icing sugar

Pepermint extract

Food colouring

Method:

1. Line baking sheet with greaseproof paper.
2. Whisk egg white until frothy.
3. Sift in icing sugar until the mixture is stiff.
4. Knead in peppermint essence and food colouring.
5. Roll mixture into balls, place on baking sheet.
6. Flatten with a fork and refrigerate for 24 hours.

Musical Munchies Song Book

Ally Bally Bee

Traditional

    C   F   C
Ally Bally, Ally Bally Bee
Am   G
Sitting on your daddy's knee
   C   F   C
Greeting for a wee penny
Am   G C
To buy some Coulter's candy

Guacamole

Ingredients:
2 ripe avocados
¼ tsp salt
1 tsp lemon juice

Method:
1. Slice avocados in half around the pip.
2. Remove pip and scoop the fruit out of the skin.
3. Using a fork, mash fruit to an even consistency.
4. Add salt and lemon juice and mix well.
5. Serve with corn crisps and tortillas, accompanied with salsa and sour cream.

Frances Turnbull

Traditional

C
Round and round

The wheel goes round

Am
As it goes the

C
Corn is ground

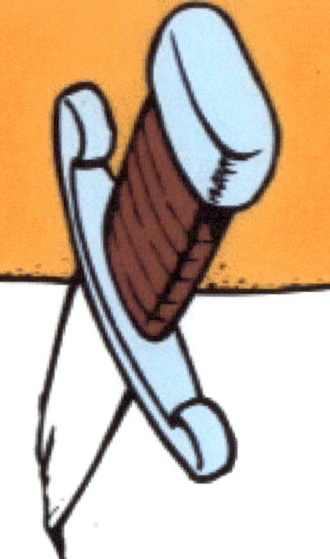

Rainbow Cous Cous Salad

Ingredients:

50g cous cous

100ml vegetable stock

1 spring onions

1/2 red pepper

1/4 cucumber

25g feta cheese cubes

2 tablespoons pesto

Method:

1. Pour cous cous into a large bowl with stock.
2. Cover, leave for 10 minutes until fluffy.
3. Slice onions and peppers, dice cucumbers.
4. Add these to couscous and fork through pesto.
5. Crumble in feta cheese.
6. Sprinkle optional pine nuts to serve.

Musical Munchies Song Book

Jolly Miller

Traditional

      C   F   G
There was a jolly miller and he lived by himself
      C   G   C
When the wheel went round he made his wealth
   C   F   G
With one hand in his pocket and the other in his bag
      C   G   C
When the wheel went round he made his grab

Lemonade

Ingredients:
¾-1 cup of sugar
1 cup of water
1 cup of lemon juice
3-4 cups of cold water (dilute)

Method:
1. Make simple syrup by heating the sugar and water in a small saucepan until the sugar is dissolved completely.
2. While the sugar is dissolving, use a juicer to extract the juice from 4 to 6 lemons, enough for one cup of juice.
3. Add the juice and the sugar water to a pitcher.
4. Add 3 to 4 cups of cold water, more or less to the desired strength.
5. Refrigerate 30 to 40 minutes. If the lemonade is a little sweet for your taste, add a little more straight lemon juice to it.
6. Serve with ice and sliced lemons. Serves 6.

Frances Turnbull

Traditional

C
Here we come! Where from?
C
Bolton! What's your trade?
Am   **F**
Cotton mills and lemonade!
G   **C**
Give us some if you're not afraid!

Lime and Kiwi Mocktail

Ingredients:

1/2 cup lime juice

sugar (for dusting)

4 kiwi fruits (peeled, keep 4 slices)

2 tablespoons of honey

1 bottle soda water

Method:

1. Place a little lime juice in a saucer and dip top of 4 cups/glasses.
2. Place sugar in a saucer and dip top of cups/glasses.
3. Mash kiwi fruit with lime juice and honey.
4. Stir in soda water and chill.
5. Serve in sugar-topped cups/glasses and decorate with a slice of kiwi fruit on the side of the cup/glass.

Musical Munchies Song Book

    C   Am   G   C   *Traditional*
Ten green bottles hanging on the wall
    C   Am   G   C
Ten green bottles hanging on the wall
   F   C   F   G
If one green bottle should accidentally fall
     C   Am   G   C
There'll be nine green bottles hanging on the wall

Fish Cakes

Ingredients:

1 small chopped onion
500g fish fillets
350ml fish stock
fresh/dry breadcrumbs
500g mashed potato
chopped parsley
flour for dusting
1 beaten egg
oil for frying

Method:

1. Simmer onion, fish and stock for 6-8 min.
2. Strain out onion and sauce.
3. Mix fish with mashed potato and herbs.
4. Shape into fish cakes and dust with flour.
5. Dip into egg, then dip into breadcrumbs.
6. Chill for 30-60 min and fry lightly 3-4 min each side.
7. Serve warm with peas and parsley sauce.

Frances Turnbull

Traditional

   C
Ickle Ockle blue bottle

   C
Fishes in the sea

Am   F
If you want a partner

G   C
Just choose me

Toad in the Hole

Ingredients:

8 sausages

1 tablespoon oil

225g plain flour

4 eggs

250g milk

salt and pepper to taste

Method:

1. Preheat oven to 200°C.
2. Pour oil in baking pan, arrange sausages and bake for 10 minutes.
3. Whisk flour, eggs, milk into batter, season.
4. Remove sausages from oven, pour batter into pan around sausages.
5. Return pan to oven for 35 min until top is crispy, bottom is soft.

Musical Munchies Song Book

Five Fat Sausages

Traditional

C
Five fat sausages sizzling in a pan

C
Five fat sausages sizzling in a pan

Am   **F**
One went pop and then went bang

G   **C**
Four fat sausages sizzling a pan

Toffee Apples

Ingredients:

4 Granny Smith apples

200g folder caster sugar

1/2 teaspoon vinegar

2 tablespoons golden syrup

sugar thermometer

Method:

1. Cover apples in boiling water and dry thoroughly.
2. Twist off stalks and push a wooden skewer into each apple.
3. Add sugar to pan, 100ml water at medium heat.
4. Cook for 5 min, stir in vinegar and syrup.
5. Use sugar thermometer to boil to 140°C or "hard crack" stage (alternatively, drop in cold water and see if it will break easily).
6. Dip and twist each apple into the toffee and leave to harden.

Frances Turnbull

Apple Tree

Traditional

C
Apple tree, apple tree
C
Will your apple fall on me
Am   F
I won't cry and I won't shout
G   C
If your apple knocks me out

Fruit smoothies

Ingredients:

1 1/2 cups apple juice
1 ripe peach (peeled, pitted, chopped)
1 ripe banana (peeled and chopped)
1 tablespoon vanilla yoghurt
6 ice cubes
2 teaspoons honey

Method:

1. Peel and take out the pit of the peach and chop.
2. Peel and chop the banana.
3. Add all the ingredients to a blender and puree until smooth.
4. Pour into glasses and serve straight away.

Apple Peaches

Traditional

Apples, peaches, pears, plums

Tell me when your birthday comes

January, February, March and April, May

June, July and August, September and October

November and December

That's my birthday!

Hot Cross Buns

Ingredients:

250g bread flour	3.5g instant yeast
1/4 teaspoon salt	100g mixed dried fruit
1 teaspoon mixed spice	100ml milk
25g caster sugar	1 egg
25g butter	1 1/2 tablespoons plain flour
	honey/syrup for brushing

Method:

1. Mix bread flour, salt, spice and sugar.
2. Rub in butter, stir in dried fruit, sprinkle yeast.
3. Warm milk, beat in egg, and mix with ingredients to form a dough.
4. Cut dough into 8 pieces, mould into buns, cover loosely with cling film and leave in a warm place for 45 min to rise.
5. Heat oven to 220°C and mix plain flour with a tablespoon of water in a plastic bag to make paste.
6. Cut small hole in bag, form cross on buns.
7. Bake for 12-15 min, brush over with honey/syrup.

Frances Turnbull

Hot Cross Buns

Traditional

      C   Am
Hot cross buns, hot cross buns

  C   G   C
One a penny, two a penny, hot cross buns

Am   G   F   G
If you have no daughters, give them to your sons

  Am   G   C
One a penny, two a penny, hot cross buns

Chelsea Buns

Ingredients:

250g strong flour	*Filling*
1/2 teaspoon salt	12.5g butter
20g butter	30g brown sugar
3.5g instant yeast	1 teaspoon cinnamon
150ml milk	75g dried mixed fruit
1/2 egg	2 tablespoons milk/sugar

Method:

1. Mix bread flour, salt and yeast.
2. Warm milk and butter in pan, cool, beat in egg and knead into dry ingredients.
3. Place dough in oiled bowl, cover loosely with cling film, leave in warm place for 60 min to rise.
4. Knead dough down again, roll into rectangle.
5. Brush with butter, sprinkle sugar, fruit, cinnamon.
6. Roll dough into cylinder-shape and cut 4cm slices.
7. Place on baking tray, cover, allow to rise for 30 min.
8. Preheat over to 190°C, bake for 20-25 min.
9. To make glaze, heat milk and sugar until boiling, brush buns after baked.

Traditional

    C   G
5 currant buns in a baker's shop
G   C
Big and round with a cherry on top
C   G
Along came a girl with a penny one day
G   C
Bought a currant bun and took it away

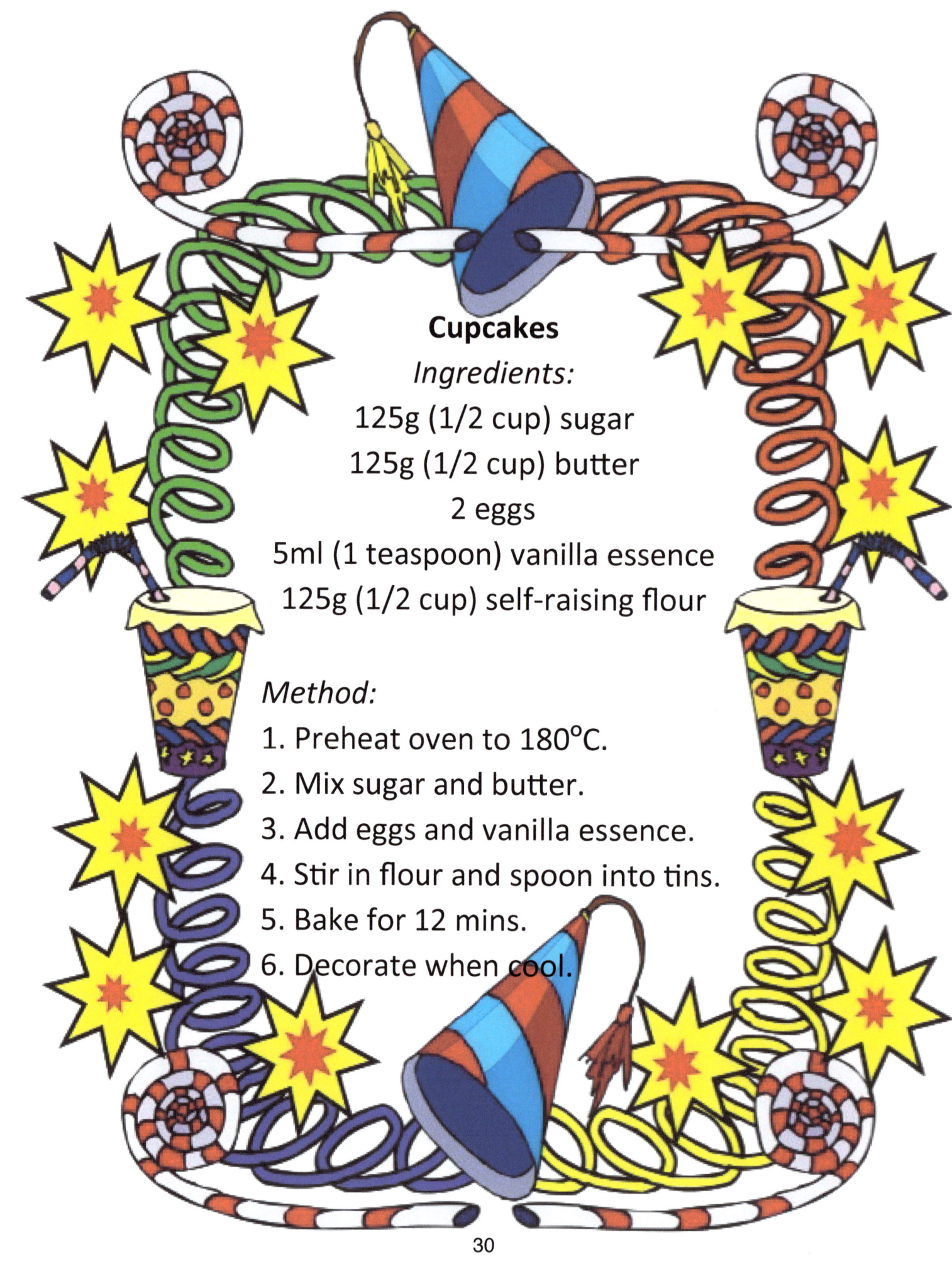

Cupcakes

Ingredients:

125g (1/2 cup) sugar

125g (1/2 cup) butter

2 eggs

5ml (1 teaspoon) vanilla essence

125g (1/2 cup) self-raising flour

Method:

1. Preheat oven to 180°C.
2. Mix sugar and butter.
3. Add eggs and vanilla essence.
4. Stir in flour and spoon into tins.
5. Bake for 12 mins.
6. Decorate when cool.

Traditional

C
Come butter come

C
Come butter come

G
Mary sits at the gate

G
Waiting for a butter cake

Banana Nut Muffins

Ingredients:

200g flour

1 1/2 teaspoons baking powder

1/4 teaspoons bicarbonate of soda

1/8 teaspoons salt

150g caster sugar

2 egg whites

225g mashed banana

3 tablespoons oil

4 tablespoons chopped walnuts

Method:

1. Preheat oven to 180°C, grease muffin tin.
2. Stir flour, baking powder, soda and salt.
3. Beat egg whites, stir in bananas, sugar, oil.
4. Add to flour mixture and walnuts.
5. Fill muffins tins two thirds, and bake for 20-25 min.

Frances Turnbull

Traditional

   C
Do you know the muffin man
  F   G
the muffin man, the muffin man
  C   Am
Do you know the muffin man
  G   C
Who lives on Drury Lane?

Children's Sangria

Ingredients:

Ice
Jug of water
Oranges and lemons
Ginger ale/club soda

Method:

1. Fill jug with water.
2. Slice or dice fruit, remove seeds and add fruits and juice from fruits to water.
3. Chill overnight.
4. Add ginger ale or club soda before serving.
5. Serve over ice.

Musical Munchies Song Book

Oranges & Lemons

Traditional

| C | Am | G | C |

"Oranges and lemons," say the bells of St Clements

| C | Am | G | C |

"I owe you two farthing," say the bells of St Martins

| C | Am | G | C |

"When will you pay me," say the bells of Old Bailey

| C | Am | G | C |

"When I grow rich," say the bells of Shoreditch

| C | Am | G | C |

"When will that be," say the bells of Stepney

| C | Am | G | C |

"I do not know," says the great bell of Bow

Summer fruit salad

Ingredients:

1 Papaya

1 Mango

2 Kiwis

2 Bananas

1/4 cup orange/tropical juice

Method:

1. Peel and chop the papaya and place in bowl.
2. Peel and chop the mango and add to bowl.
3. Peel and chop the kiwis and add to bowl.
4. Peel and chop the bananas and add to bowl.
5. Add orange or tropical juice and serve.

Frances Turnbull

Traditional

C
Where oh where is pretty little Susie

G
Where oh where is pretty little Susie

Am
Where oh where is pretty little Susie

G **C**
Way down yonder on the paw paw patch

Buttermilk Pancakes

Ingredients:

1 1/3 cup flour

3 tablespoons sugar

1 teaspoon baking powder

1 teaspoon bicarbonate of soda

1 teaspoon salt

2 large eggs

1 1/4 cups buttermilk

2 tablespoons melted butter

Method:

1. Whisk dry ingredients together.
2. Whisk eggs, butter and buttermilk and stir into dry ingredients, forming a batter.
3. Heat frying pan, brush with oil.
4. Pour batter into pan, covering the base.
5. When bubbles appear on the top of the pancake, flip it over.
6. Repeat until batter is finished.

Skip to my Lou

Traditional

C **G**
Skip, skip, skip to my Lou, skip, skip, skip to my Lou
Am **G** **C**
Skip, skip, skip to my Lou, skip to my Lou, my darling

C
Fly in the buttermilk, shoo fly shoo
G
Fly in the buttermilk, shoo fly shoo
Am
Fly in the buttermilk, shoo fly shoo
G **C**
Skip to my Lou, my darling

Pumpkin Pie

Ingredients:

750g pumpkin chunks

350g short crust pastry

140g caster sugar

1/2 teaspoon salt, nutmeg, cinnamon

2 eggs

25g butter

175 ml milk

Method:

1. Boil pumpkin for 15 min or until tender and cool.
2. Line 22cm tart tin with rolled pastry
3. Bake blind at 180°C for 15 min until golden brown.
4. Purée pumpkin and add dry ingredients.
5. Pour in pastry shell and cook for 10 min at 220°C.
6. Reduce to 180°C and continue baking for 35 min.
7. Cool and remove from tin.
8. Sprinkle with cinnamon sugar, serve chilled.

Frances Turnbull

Pumpkin Pumpkin

Traditional

    C
Pumpkin, pumpkin
        G
Round and fat
C
Turns into a jack o' lantern
     G   C
Just like that

Pease Pudding

Ingredients:

Pack of bacon

Salt and pepper

475g split peas

Method:

1. Place split peas in large ovenproof dish.
2. Cover with water, 475g of split peas to every 2 litres of water, adding salt and pepper to season.
3. Allow to stand overnight.
4. Add small pieces of chopped bacon (not the fat or rind) into mixture.
5. Place on middle shelf of oven, gas mark 5 or 150°C.
6. Cook until set, medium consistency (not too thick or thin as once cool it sets even thicker).
7. Eat hot or cold, spread onto fresh bread and butter.

Traditional

[C]Pease pudding hot, pease pudding co[G]ld
[Am]Pease pu[C]dding in the pot nine [G]days [C]old
[C]Some like it hot, some like it co[G]ld
[Am]Some li[C]ke it in the pot nine [G]days [C]old

Vegetable Stew
Ingredients:
1 onion, chopped
1 cup (250g) barley
Mushroom ketchup or vegetable stock cube with water
½ cup oats
1 tin of peas
1 tin of kidney beans
Salt and pepper to taste

Method:
1. Lightly fry one chopped onion.
2. Once golden brown, add mushroom ketchup or stock and barley, and simmer on low for 30 minutes.
3. Add the tinned peas, beans and dry porridge oats with salt and pepper to taste.
4. Cook on low-medium for a final 10 minutes and serve hot or cold with rice, potatoes or dumplings.

Frances Turnbull

Oats, Peas, Beans

Traditional

 C
Oats, peas, beans and barley grow
 G
Oats, peas, beans and barley grow
      Am
Not you nor I nor anyone knows how
 G   C
Oats, peas, beans and barley grow

My Song: _____

www.musicaliti.co.uk

**Magical Musical Kingdom
Ukulele Song Book
ISBN 9781907935770**
Follow the story of King Crotchet and Queen Quaver, and play along on your ukulele!

**Magical Musical Kingdom
Ukulele Song Book
ISBN 9781907935770**
Sing about all types of animals, and play along on your ukulele!

**Come and Sing 1
FREE iBook
ISBN 9781907935640**
7 nursery songs are presented in this ibook. Using the Musicaliti skill sequence, develop musical skills using children's songs.

**Magical Musical Kingdom
Nursery Lesson Planner
ISBN 9781907935152**
This nursery planner walks teachers through 10-12 complete music lessons for 2-4 year olds about royalty and magic.

**Yum, Yum, Yum!
Nursery Lesson Planner
ISBN 9781907935206**
This nursery planner walks teachers through 10-12 complete music lessons for 2-4 year olds about food.

**Goodies for Guitar
Guitar Tutor Book
ISBN 9781907935695**
90 songs for beginners on guitar. Learn about music beats and notes by singing fun songs like Hot Cross Buns and Twinkle Twinkle!

Follow *Musicaliti* on Blogger, FaceBook, LInkedIn, Pinterest, ReverbNation, SoundCloud, Twitter, Wordpress and YouTube

ABOUT THE AUTHOR

Frances has presented early years music sessions in a variety of settings since 2006, after training as a secondary mathematics and science teacher. She is involved in research into the health, educational and developmental benefits of music. Seeing the musical links between the ages, she delivers music sessions in care homes, trains early years trainee students, and directs a local community choir, the Bolton Warblers.

www.ingramcontent.com/pod-product-compliance
Lightning Source LLC
Chambersburg PA
CBHW041534040426
42446CB00002B/85